Chocolate Truffles

by Carrie Huber

WRC PUBLISHING

Cookbooks Make Great Gifts

WRC Publishing has a variety of specialty cookbooks. If your local cookware/gourmet shop does not carry any of our titles, we will be happy to send you a free catalog of our books.

For information on all our books send a self-addressed stamped envelope to:

WRC Publishing
Attn: Order Department
P.O. Box 2691-BK
Silver Spring, MD 20902

Announcing!
The American Cooking Guild

Who belongs in The American Cooking Guild? Anyone who'd rather be in the kitchen than in any other room of the house!

Imagine saving 10% to 40% off all the new cookware and gourmet products that you want today! Imagine receiving free cookbooks! Imagine being part of a monthly national exchange of cooking ideas, recipes, news, trends and more as you receive our monthly newsletter, *Something's Cooking.*

Well, you don't have to imagine because now you can do all these things—and much more—as a member of The American Cooking Guild!

FOR MORE INFORMATION, SEND INQUIRIES TO: The American Cooking Guild, Membership Office, 2915 Fenimore Road, Silver Spring, MD 20902.

Acknowledgements
—Edited by Sheilah Kaufman
—Cover Photograph by John Burwell
—Cover Design by Bill Cates and Jim Haynes

Published by:
WRC Publishing
2915 Fenimore Road
P.O. Box 2691
Silver Spring, MD 20902
301-949-6787

Table of Contents

Non-Alcoholic Truffles

Introduction

Chocolate Truffles is a comprehensive guide to the history, preparation and appreciation of that most exalted of all candies, the Chocolate Truffle. While I've attempted to write for the home chef without prior candy making experience, this book contains tips and recipes that should also be of interest to the sophisticated confectioner. This book grew out of my frustration at being unable to find adequate publications on the subject of Chocolate Truffles.

There were numerous books on chocolate, however any references to truffles they contained were incorrectly named fudge squares, or other more common candies. Assuming that others shared my frustration, I researched the subject thoroughly, conducted extensive kitchen tests based on the few traditional recipes I had culled from existing sources, and modified or invented these truffle recipes.

I've tried to keep in mind that many of you, like myself, are not formally-trained chefs, and may wrongly feel that one needs a degree from the Cordon Bleu before one can think about making chocolate truffles.

Actually, it's quite simple to create fine chocolates at home. All that is necessary is time, the right equipment and ingredients, a love of fine chocolates, and a group of family or friends who share your sweet tooth. Once you try it, you'll wonder why you waited this long to join the ranks of the home chocolatier. Good luck, and welcome!

What is a Truffle?

Named for its lumpy resemblance to the Perigord truffle of France, a Chocolate Truffle is technically any candy center either dipped or rolled, freeform, in chocolate coating or powder. Since this is a rather broad category, there are some oddball candies floating around that go by the generic name of "truffle".

When I speak of truffles, I mean the incomparable chocolate delight that stands above any other kind of candy. The True Truffle is huge, often nearly the size of a golfball. Regardless of its particular flavor or coating, it contains the sinfully silky rich chocolate cream center called "Ganache". These are the true royalty of the chocolate world. Also included are recipes which substitute fresh buttercream, (either wholly or in part), for the ganache center, in the belief that these truffles are sometimes equally as marvelous. I hope you agree.

For all their delicacy, Chocolate Truffles really aren't difficult to make at home. It takes some time, some basic equipment, the very best ingredients, and a little attention to detail. The results are spectacular and well worth the effort.

Fear of Chocolate

Perhaps you've heard frightening stories about working with chocolate. Well, believe me, they're all true. However, there are some very easy rules for working with chocolate which can transform its temperamental nature into a model of sweet predictability.

The Three Commandments of Chocolate

1. Avoid Water

Never allow water (or steam) not even the smallest drop, to get into a pan of chocolate. Try it once and you'll discover why; the chocolate will stiffen and become lumpy, making it necessary to throw out the whole batch and start over. Make sure all pans and utensils are perfectly dry before touching chocolate.

2. Avoid Humidity

Try to choose a cool, dry day to make candy, for the above-stated reasons. If it's rainy or humid out, forget it. Moisture in the air or on your spoon is chocolate's mortal enemy. Make sure the room is cool and has no drafts or direct sunlight, or the candies will develop gray streaks and lose their sheen.

3. Avoid High Heat

Never subject chocolate to high heat, as it scorches very easily. Melt chocolate at a steady heat, (no hotter than 110°F) stirring constantly to keep the cocoa butter evenly distributed. If not, the chocolate can become discolored, developing what is known as "bloom."

Melting Chocolate

The most foolproof method for melting chocolate, and the only one I recommend, is as follows:
Chop or grate chocolate into small pieces, working with 1-2 pounds of chocolate at a time. (Less than one pound or more than two pounds is too hard to work with at one time, and will not melt evenly.) Place the chocolate pieces into the top half of a double boiler. Put very hot water in the bottom half of the double boiler, without letting the top pan touch the water. Let the chocolate sit until it begins to melt, then stir until smooth.

There are three other methods of melting chocolate, which I'll list in order of descending reliability:
1. Put grated chocolate into a microwave oven. Set the oven on high power for two minutes. Promptly remove from oven and stir until smooth.
2. Place a bowl of grated chocolate in a turned-off but still warm oven. Check constantly to insure that it doesn't burn. Stir until smooth.
3. Put grated chocolate in a small, heavy saucepan over a very low heat, stirring constantly. Don't blame me if it burns; the stovetop method is definitely not recommended. If you use it, you're on your own.

What Types of Chocolate to Use?

Traditionally, dark sweet chocolate (also called bitter-sweet) has been the confectioner's choice for dipping due to its delicious flavor and dark, glossy appearance. It is slightly harder to work with than semisweet or milk chocolate. An acceptable alternative to pure dark chocolate in most dipping recipes is an equal blend of dark and semi-sweet chocolate. Of course, the flavor is somewhat sweeter, but it too has a rich and lovely color and is easier to work with. Another possibility is white chocolate, which complements many truffle recipes beautifully and acts as a silky, cream-colored counterpoint to a tray filled with dark candies.

Dipping

Dipping is a more exacting process than preparing ganache. The temperature and texture of the chocolate are fairly critical.

With the dipping chocolate, it's recommended to stay with only the three aforementioned chocolates. However, the chocolate ganache can include whatever type of chocolate you prefer; dark sweet, semisweet, milk chocolate, or white.

All of these can be purchased in chunks or by the pound from any candy supply source. The truly superior brands of imported chocolate must be purchased in precut blocks of varying weight. Good quality truffles can also be made from the more common domestic chunk chocolate that is usually found in candy supply stores. A partial list of mail order outlets for chocolate and chocolate-making supplies is listed later in this section.

Preparation

Having prepared your ganache, buttercream or other filling at least a day ahead*, you are now ready to begin making truffles. Gather all your equipment around you as follows:

- The double boiler
- Wooden spoon for stirring
- Dipping fork or bon bon dipper (a fondue or kitchen fork also works)
- Candy or Bi-Therm thermometer with a range of 80°-130°F
- Baking sheet(s) covered with waxed or parchment paper.

Chocolate ganache and buttercream are both made with fresh, heavy cream and sometimes butter and eggs as well. Chocolate Truffles are very perishable and must be refrigerated at all times. Use the freshest possible dairy items in your truffles, and plan to use them within two weeks. There are few things in life more disappointing than a big bite of a rancid truffle.

If it is absolutely necessary, you can store leftovers in the freezer for a week or two longer, but it does nothing to improve the flavor.

*This delay allows the candy to harden enough to be workable. If there is alcohol in the recipe, it uses this time to ripen as well.

Dusting Truffles

The following truffle recipes can substitute cocoa powder dusting for the fresh chocolate dipping. In my opinion dusted truffles aren't quite as special as the chocolate dipped kind. Their advantage, however, is that they are far quicker and easier to mass produce.

This is the basic method for dusting truffles:
When the ganache is formed into balls and placed on a baking sheet, put baking sheet in the freezer instead of the refrigerator. When frozen you may put 15-20 truffles at a time in a plastic bag with 2 Tablespoons unsweetened cocoa powder, preferably Dutch® process. Shake bag to coat evenly, then repeat with remaining truffles. Arrange truffles once again on waxed paper-lined baking sheet, and refrigerate as you would other truffles.

Whoops!

Salvaging those chocolate tragedies.

Many things can go wrong when you work with chocolate, but it's my belief that the project is hardly ever truly ruined. If you follow directions carefully chocolate mishaps should not occur, however at times disaster strikes even the most careful confectioner. Here are a few things that I do when my truffles are in trouble:

1. Stiffened Chocolate

An unseen speck of water in the pan? Or perhaps you unthinkingly added liqueur or other liquid before the melted chocolate cooled to room temperature? Adding vegetable oil to the brew often alleviates the situation. Add it by ¼ cup increments, stirring thoroughly each time, and keep your fingers crossed.

2. Ganache Refuses to Harden

This is a tricky one. Some recipes harden in 2 hours, others are still soft after 2 days. If ganache remains too soft to form into balls, I dig it out of the bowl by the teaspoonful and push it with a finger onto the baking sheet. Usually, with a minimum of patting, it takes a truffle-like shape. I then freeze the baking sheet several hours or overnight, to achieve the necessary consistency for dipping or dusting.

3. Holes in the Truffle's Coat

Somehow you missed a spot when you were dipping—the ganache is peeking through. Using either your finger or a new paintbrush, brush a bit of warm chocolate over the area. You can do a first-rate patch job, with nobody the wiser.

4. Left-over Dipping Chocolate

Sometimes you will have left-over chocolate from the dipping process. Mix it with raisins, nuts, coconut, or a combination of ingredients to form drop candy clusters. You can also dip fresh fruit into this chocolate.

Where To Find It

Most of the tools and ingredients specified in this book can be found in any gourmet kitchen shop or candymaking specialty store. If you'd prefer to shop by mail, here are two excellent sources for dipping chocolates, dipping forks, candy thermometers, fluted paper candy cups, gift boxes and various other candy making accessories. The catalogs are available free from:

Madame Chocolate
1940-C Lehigh Avenue
Glenview, IL 60025
Telephone 312/729-3330

or

Simply Chocolate
PO Box 16037
St. Paul, MN 55116
Telephone 612/690-4322

Other possible mail order sources include the following gourmet mail order catalogs. While not specifically dedicated to the needs of the chocolatier, these free catalogs are worth a look:

Williams-Sonoma
Mail Order Dept.
PO Box 7456
San Francisco, CA 94120-7456
Telephone 415/652-9007

Chef's Catalog
3915 Commercial Avenue
Northbrook, IL 60062
Telephone 312/480-9400

The Ervan Guttman, Co.
8206 Blue Ash Road
Cincinnati, OH 45236

Figi's Collection for Cooking
Marshfield, WI 54449

The Basic Truffle
& Variations

The Basic Chocolate Truffle

> 8 ounces dark sweet chocolate
> 1 cup heavy cream, room temperature

Chocolate Coating:
> 16 ounces dark sweet chocolate
> ¼ cup vegetable oil

Making the Ganache

To prepare ganache, chop or grate chocolate into small pieces. Place in top half of double boiler along with cream. Put hot (not boiling) water in bottom half of a double boiler, making sure the water doesn't touch the top pan. Stir often with wooden spoon. When all of the chocolate has melted, beat until well combined. Remove from heat, let cool to room temperature. Transfer to covered bowl and refrigerate overnight to harden. (Ganache will keep in this state for a few days if necessary.)

Take a little ganache at a time and form 1" balls, using fingertips (with as little contact as possible so the chocolate doesn't soften). Keep unused portion refrigerated as you work. Place balls on waxed paper-lined baking sheet; continue until ganache is used up. Refrigerate baking sheet until ganache is hardened, overnight or up to two days. Allow to set in the refrigerator at least two hours before loosely covering with waxed paper.*

Prepare Chocolate Coating:

Chop or grate chocolate into small pieces. Heat chocolate and oil together in top of double boiler over hot water, stirring until smooth with a wooden spoon. Insert candy thermometer and begin dipping the ganache balls when temperature registers between 85°-90°F. If chocolate begins to cool and thicken before you're finished dipping, reheat over hot water. Work with only ½ dozen at a time, keeping the rest refrigerated. Drop a single ganache ball into the chocolate, turning to coat well, then lift it with the fork. Allow excess chocolate to drip back into pan, then gently rap fork against edge of pan to remove more chocolate from ball. Failure to do this will cause a large dribbly "platform" or "skirt" to form around the base of each hardened truffle. (This makes it difficult to pack them side by side in a box.)

There are two schools of thought as to the proper method of depositing truffles onto the baking sheet: A) If you are conservative by nature it's best to gently slide them off the fork with a butterknife, onto the waiting baking sheet. B) If you intend to further decorate the truffle, the second method, (for the showoffs among us) involves dropping the truffle off the fork upside down directly onto the baking sheet. Quickly manipulate the single strand of chocolate, adhering to the fork, into some glorious shape atop the candy, like the pros do. Either way is acceptable, although the second way requires some practice and an accurate thermometer to get it right. If your chocolate temperature is off by a few degrees, you're likely to find a chocolate highway not a chocolate strand adhering to the fork when that critical moment comes.

I generally use the first method largely because it's easier, but also because I prefer to further decorate my truffles into miniature works of art. The perfect finale for the basic recipe, for instance, is a sprinkling of shaved dark chocolate over the top, or better yet, gently rolling each newly-dipped truffle in the shavings to coat completely.

Refrigerate all truffles after dipping several hours or overnight to harden.

*Foil can be substituted in all cases for waxed paper, but never use clear plastic wrap. It clings too tightly to the candies and traps moisture inside which discolors the chocolate.

For Gift Packing: Find a candy box or tin large enough to hold a single layer of truffles. Line with foil. Fill box with truffles (fluted candy cups are optional), cover tightly and refrigerate until ready to present.

Variations on Basic Truffle

Variation 1 — Bavarian Mint Truffles

Ganache
- 8 ounces dark sweet chocolate
- ¾ cup heavy cream
- 1½ Tablespoons Creme De Menthe

Dipping
- 16 ounces dark sweet chocolate
- ¼ cup vegetable oil

Garnish
- green sprinkles for garnish

When chocolate and cream ganache have cooled to room temperature, stir in Creme De Menthe before refrigerating.

Sprinkle dipped truffles with green sprinkles.

Variation 2 — Cream Sherry Truffles

Ganache
- 8 ounces dark sweet chocolate
- ⅔ cup heavy cream
- 2 Tablespoons Bristol Cream Sherry®

Dipping
- 16 ounces dark sweet chocolate
- ¼ cup vegetable oil

Garnish
- 2 cups chocolate shavings

When ganache has cooled to room temperature, stir in sherry before refrigerating.

Roll dipped truffle in chocolate shavings.

Variation 3 — Dark Rum Truffles

Ganache
- 8 ounces dark sweet chocolate
- ⅔ cup heavy cream
- 2½ Tablespoons dark rum
- ¼ teaspoon lime juice

Dipping
- 16 ounces dark sweet chocolate
- ¼ cup vegetable oil

Garnish
- slivered lime peel

When ganache has cooled to room temperature, add rum and lime juice before refrigerating.

Top dipped truffle with slivers of lime peel.

Variation 4 — Bourbon Pecan Truffles

Ganache
- 8 ounces dark sweet chocolate
- ¾ cup heavy cream
- 1½ Tablespoons bourbon
- ½ cup chopped pecans

Dipping
- 16 ounces dark sweet chocolate
- ¼ cup vegetable oil

Garnish
- 1 cup whole pecans

When ganache has cooled to room temperature, fold in bourbon and chopped pecans before refrigerating.

Top dipped truffle with a whole pecan.

Variation 5 — Amaretto Truffles

Ganache
- 8 ounces dark sweet chocolate
- ¾ cup heavy cream
- 1½ Tablespoons Amaretto

Dipping
- 16 ounces dark sweet chocolate
- ¼ cup vegetable oil

Garnish
- 2 cups chopped almonds

When ganache has cooled to room temperature, add Amaretto.

Roll dipped truffle in chopped almonds.

Variation 6 — Kahlua Cream Truffles

Ganache
- 8 ounces dark sweet chocolate
- ¾ cup heavy cream
- 2 Tablespoons Kahlua®

Dipping
- 16 ounces dark sweet chocolate
- ¼ cup vegetable oil

Garnish
- 1 cup chocolate coffee beans

When ganache has cooled to room temperature add Kahlua before refrigerating.

Top dipped truffle with a chocolate coffee bean.

Variation 7 — Irish Cream Truffles

Ganache
- 8 ounces semisweet chocolate
- ¾ cup heavy cream
- ¼ cup Irish Cream Liqueu

Dipping
- 16 ounces dark sweet chocolate
- ¼ cup vegetable oil

Garnish
- 2 cups chocolate sprinkles

When ganache is room temperature, add Irish Cream before refrigerating.

Roll dipped truffle in chocolate sprinkles.

Variation 8 — Grand Marnier Truffles

Ganache
- 9 ounces dark sweet chocolate
- 1 cup heavy cream
- 2 Tablespoons sweet butter
- 1½ Tablespoons Grand Marnier®

Dipping
- 16 ounces white chocolate
- ¼ cup vegetable oil

Garnish
- candied orange peel

Melt chocolate, cream and butter together. When cool, add Grand Marnier before refrigerating.

Top dipped truffle with candied orange peel.

Variation 9 — Pistachio Truffles

Ganache
- 9 ounces semisweet chocolate
- 1 cup heavy cream
- 2 Tablespoons sweet butter
- 1½ Tablespoons Pistacha Pistachio Liqueur®

Dipping
- 16 ounces white chocolate
- ¼ cup vegetable oil

Garnish
- 1 cup chopped pistachios

Melt chocolate, cream, and butter together. When cool, stir in Pistacha Pistachio Liqueur before refrigerating.

Top dipped truffle with sprinkled chopped nuts.

Spirited Truffles

Tropical Truffles

A truffle reminiscent of tall cool drinks on hot sandy beaches.

> 9 *ounces semisweet chocolate*
> ½ *cup heavy cream, room temperature*
> 1 *Tablespoon pineapple juice*
> ⅛ *teaspoon grenadine*
> 1 *Tablespoon dark rum*

Chocolate Coating:
> 16 *ounces dark sweet chocolate*
> ¼ *cup vegetable oil*
> 2 *cups shredded coconut*

 ## Ganache

Prepare ganache by chopping or grating chocolate into small pieces. Place in top half of double boiler along with cream. Put hot, (not boiling) water in bottom of double boiler, taking care that water doesn't touch top half. Stir with a wooden spoon. When melted, beat vigorously until smooth. Remove from heat and let cool to room temperature.

When ganache is at room temperature, add pineapple juice, grenadine and rum. Stir until thoroughly blended. Transfer to a covered bowl and refrigerate overnight or until hardened.

Taking a little ganache at a time, form 1" balls using fingertips (with minimal contact so chocolate doesn't soften). Keep unused portion refrigerated as you work. Place balls on waxed paper-lined baking sheet and refrigerate overnight until truffles are hardened. Allow to set in refrigerator at least 2 hours before loosely covering with waxed paper.

Dipping

Prepare chocolate coating with 16 ounces dark sweet chocolate and ¼ cup vegetable oil. Chop or grate chocolate into small pieces. Heat chocolate and oil together in top of double boiler over hot water, stirring with a wooden spoon until smooth. Insert candy thermometer and begin dipping ganache balls when temperature registers between 85°-90°F. If chocolate begins to cool and thicken before you're finished dipping, reheat over hot water.

Work with ½ dozen ganache balls at a time, keeping the rest refrigerated. Drop ganache ball into the chocolate, turning until completely covered. Lift with fork, letting excess drain off, then gently rap fork against rim of pan to remove more chocolate. Gently slide truffle off of fork (using a butterknife) onto waxed paper-lined baking sheet. Repeat with remaining truffles.

Garnish

Spread coconut on another waxed paper-lined surface, and gently roll each truffle in it until completely coated. Refrigerate truffles overnight or until firm. Allow to set in refrigerator at least 2 hours before loosely covering with waxed paper.

Makes approximately 2 dozen.

Brandied Raisin Truffles

A truffle for the most discriminating palate.

    6 *ounces raisins*
    ¾ *cup brandy*
    9 *ounces semisweet chocolate*
    ¾ *cup heavy cream, room temperature*
    2 *Tablespoons butter, room temperature*

Chocolate Coating:
    16 *ounces dark sweet chocolate*
    ¼ *cup vegetable oil*
    ½ *cup raisins for garnish*

 **Ganache**

Put raisins in saucepan, cover with water. Simmer for 5 minutes then drain completely. Transfer to small bowl and cover with brandy. Refrigerate for an hour, turning occasionally. Drain thoroughly and carefully pat dry.

Prepare ganache by chopping or grating chocolate into small pieces. Place in top half of double boiler along with cream and butter. Put hot (not boiling) water in bottom of double boiler, taking care that water doesn't touch top half. Stir with a wooden spoon. When melted, beat vigorously until smooth. Remove from heat and let cool to room temperature.

When ganache is at room temperature, gently fold in brandied raisins. Transfer to covered bowl and refrigerate overnight to harden.

Taking a little ganache at a time, form 1" balls using fingertips (with as little contact as possible so chocolate doesn't soften). Keep unused portion refrigerated as you work. Place balls on waxed paper-lined baking sheet and refrigerate overnight until truffles are hardened. Allow to set in refrigerator at least 2 hours before loosely covering with waxed paper.

Dipping

Prepare chocolate coating with 16 ounces dark sweet chocolate and ¼ cup vegetable oil. Chop or grate chocolate into small pieces. Heat chocolate and oil together in top of double boiler over hot water, stirring with a wooden spoon until smooth. Insert candy thermometer and begin dipping ganache balls when temperature registers between 85°-90°F. If chocolate begins to cool and thicken before you're finished dipping, reheat over hot water.

Work with ½ dozen ganache balls at a time, keeping the rest refrigerated. Drop a ganache into the chocolate, turning until completely covered. Lift with fork, letting excess drain off, then gently rap fork against rim of pan to remove more chocolate. Gently slide truffle off of fork using a butterknife onto waxed paper-lined baking sheet. Repeat with remaining truffles.

Garnish

Top each truffle with a raisin for garnish. Refrigerate truffles overnight or until firm. Allow to set in refrigerator at least 2 hours before loosely covering with waxed paper.

Makes approximately 3 dozen.

Variation — Brandied Peach Truffles

Ganache

6 ounces canned peaches, chopped
¾ cup brandy
⅛ teaspoon cinnamon
9 ounces semisweet chocolate
¾ cup heavy cream

Dipping

16 ounces dark sweet chocolate
¼ cup vegetable oil

Garnish

powdered cinnamon

Marinate peaches and cinnamon in brandy for 1 hour. Drain peaches, reserve 1 Tablespoon of marinade. When ganache is at room temperature, fold in peaches and reserved marinade.

Dip truffles and sprinkle with cinnamon.

Sherried Raspberry Truffles

The tart berries come alive with the flavors of chocolate and cream sherry.

> 6 ounces raspberries
> ¾ cup cream sherry
> 8 ounces semisweet chocolate
> ⅔ cup heavy cream, room temperature

Chocolate Coating:
> 16 ounces dark sweet chocolate
> ¼ cup vegetable oil
> 1 cup unsweetened cocoa powder,
> preferably Dutch® process

 Ganache

Wash berries, then drain and coarsely chop them. Place them in a bowl. Add sherry and refrigerate for 1 hour, turning occasionally. Drain thoroughly; carefully pat dry. Reserve 1 teaspoon of marinade.

Prepare ganache by chopping or grating chocolate into small pieces. Place in top half of double boiler along with cream. Put hot (not boiling) water in bottom of double boiler, taking care that water doesn't touch top half. Stir with a wooden spoon. When melted, beat vigorously until smooth. Remove from heat and let cool to room temperature.

When ganache is at room temperature, gently fold in raspberries and reserved marinade. Transfer to covered bowl and refrigerate overnight to harden.

Taking a little ganache at a time, form 1" balls using fingertips (with as little contact as possible so chocolate doesn't soften). Keep unused portion refrigerated as you work. Place balls on waxed paper-lined baking sheet and refrigerate overnight until truffles are hardened. Allow to set in refrigerator at least 2 hours before loosely covering with waxed paper.

 **Dipping**

Prepare chocolate coating with 16 ounces dark sweet chocolate and ¼ cup vegetable oil. Chop or grate chocolate into small pieces. Heat chocolate and oil together in top of double boiler over hot water, stirring with a wooden spoon until smooth. Insert candy thermometer and begin dipping ganache balls when temperature registers between 85⁰-90⁰F. If chocolate begins to cool and thicken before you're finished dipping, reheat over hot water.

Work with ½ dozen ganache balls at a time, keeping the rest refrigerated. Drop a single truffle into the chocolate, turning until completely covered. Lift with fork, letting excess drain off, then gently rap fork against rim of pan to remove more chocolate. Gently slide truffle off of fork (using a butterknife) onto waxed paper-lined baking sheet. Repeat with remaining truffles.

 Garnish

Garnish each truffle by dusting the top with cocoa powder. Refrigerate truffles overnight or until firm. Allow to set in refrigerator at least 2 hours before loosely covering with waxed paper.

Makes approximately 30.

Rum 'N Eggnog Truffles

A special holiday truffle that's sure to become a family tradition.

> 9 *ounces semisweet chocolate*
> ⅓ *cup heavy cream*
> ⅓ *cup eggnog*
> 1 *Tablespoon dark rum*

Chocolate Coating:
> 16 *ounces dark sweet chocolate*
> ¼ *cup vegetable oil*
> 1 *cup unsweetened cocoa powder,*
> *preferably Dutch® process*

 **Ganache**

Prepare ganache by chopping or grating chocolate into small pieces. Place in top half of double boiler along with eggnog and cream. Put hot, (not boiling) water in bottom of double boiler, making sure water doesn't touch top half. Stir with wooden spoon. When melted, beat until smooth. Remove from heat and let cool to room temperature.

When ganache is at room temperature, add rum, stirring until thoroughly blended. Transfer to covered bowl and refrigerate overnight to harden.

Taking a little ganache at a time, form 1" balls using fingertips (with as little contact as possible so chocolate doesn't soften). Keep unused portion refrigerated as you work. Place balls on waxed paper-lined baking sheet and refrigerate at least 2 hours before loosely covering with waxed paper.

 # Dipping

Prepare chocolate coating with 16 ounces dark sweet chocolate and ¼ cup vegetable oil. Chop or grate chocolate into small pieces. Heat chocolate and oil together in top of double boiler over hot water, stirring with a wooden spoon until smooth. Insert candy thermometer and begin dipping ganache balls when temperature registers between 85º-90ºF. If chocolate begins to cool and thicken before you're finished dipping, reheat over hot water.

Work with ½ dozen ganache balls at a time, keeping the rest refrigerated. Drop ganache into the chocolate, turning until completely covered. Lift with fork, letting excess drain off, then gently rap fork against rim of pan to remove more chocolate. Gently slide truffle off of fork (using a butter-knife) onto waxed paper-lined baking sheet. Repeat with remaining truffles.

 # Garnish

Garnish each truffle by dusting the top with cocoa powder. Refrigerate truffles overnight or until firm. Allow to set in refrigerator at least 2 hours before loosely covering with waxed paper.

Makes approximately 2 dozen.

Black Raspberry Buttercream Truffles

A rich, fruity truffle enhanced by the flavors of raspberry preserves and black raspberry liqueur.

          3 Tablespoons sweet butter, room temperature
       1½ cups powdered sugar
          1 Tablespoon Chambord® Black Raspberry Liqueur
          1 teaspoon grated lemon zest
          1 teaspoon raspberry preserves

Chocolate Coating:
       16 ounces dark sweet chocolate
        ¼ cup vegetable oil

 Ganache

Prepare buttercream by beating butter until creamy. Slowly add powdered sugar, lemon zest, Chambord and preserves. Beat 5 minutes, or until stiff and smooth. Refrigerate in a covered bowl overnight to harden.

Taking a little buttercream at a time, form 1" balls using fingertips (with as little contact as possible so chocolate doesn't soften). Keep unused portion refrigerated as you work. Place balls on waxed paper-lined baking sheet and refrigerate overnight until truffles are hardened. Allow to set in refrigerator at least 2 hours before loosely covering with waxed paper.

Dipping

Prepare chocolate coating with 16 ounces dark sweet chocolate and ¼ cup vegetable oil. Chop or grate chocolate into small pieces. Heat chocolate and oil together in top of double boiler over hot water, stirring with a wooden spoon until smooth. Insert candy thermometer and begin dipping ganache balls when temperature registers between 85°-90°F. If chocolate begins to cool and thicken before you're finished dipping, reheat over hot water.

Work with ½ dozen ganache balls at a time, keeping the rest refrigerated. Drop ganache into the chocolate, turning until completely covered. Lift with fork, letting excess drain off, then gently rap fork against rim of pan to remove more chocolate.

Garnish

Gently invert truffle off of fork and onto waxed paper-lined baking sheet. A string of chocolate will adhere to your fork. Quickly manipulate it into a "B" shape. Repeat with remaining truffles. Refrigerate truffles overnight or until firm. Allow to set in refrigerator at least 2 hours before loosely covering with waxed paper.

Makes approximately 2 dozen.

Double Hazelnut Truffles

This darkly rich truffle combines nuts with nut flavored liqueur for a tremendously satisfying complement of tastes.

> ½ cup hazelnuts with skins removed
> 10 ounces dark sweet chocolate
> 1 cup heavy cream, room temperature
> 2 Tablespoons sweet butter, room temperature
> 3 Tablespoons Franglico Hazelnut Liqueur®

Chocolate Coating:
> 16 ounces dark sweet chocolate
> ¼ cup vegetable oil

 **Ganache**

Coarsely chop ¼ cup of hazelnuts. Store remaining ¼ cup nuts in covered container in the refrigerator. These will be used for garnish.

Prepare ganache by chopping or grating chocolate into small pieces. Place in top half of double boiler along with cream and butter. Put hot, (not boiling) water in bottom of double boiler, making sure water doesn't touch top half. Stir often with wooden spoon. When melted, beat until smooth. Remove from heat and cool to room temperature.

When ganache is at room temperature, stir in Frangelico until thoroughly blended. Transfer to covered bowl and refrigerate overnight.

Taking a little ganache at a time, form 1" balls using fingertips (with as little contact as possible so chocolate doesn't soften). Keep unused portion refrigerated as you work. Place balls on waxed paper-lined baking sheet and refrigerate overnight or until truffles are hardened. Allow to set in refrigerator at least 2 hours before loosely covering with waxed paper.

 Dipping

Sprinkle tops of ganache balls with chopped hazelnuts, pressing them in lightly with a finger to insure that they will adhere during dipping.

Prepare chocolate coating with 16 ounces dark sweet chocolate and ¼ cup vegetable oil. Chop or grate chocolate into small pieces. Heat chocolate and oil together in top of double boiler over hot water, stirring with a wooden spoon until smooth. Insert candy thermometer and begin dipping the ganache balls when temperature registers between 85⁰-90⁰F. If chocolate begins to cool and thicken before you're finished dipping, reheat over hot water.

Work with ½ dozen ganache balls at a time, keeping the rest refrigerated. Drop ganache into the chocolate, turning until completely covered. Lift with fork, letting excess drain off, then gently rap fork against edge of pan to remove more chocolate. Gently slide truffle off of fork (with a butterknife) onto waxed paper-lined baking sheet. Repeat with remaining truffles.

 Garnish

Now drop an individual hazelnut into chocolate and place on top of truffle. Repeat until all are used up.* Return baking sheet to refrigerator overnight or until firm. Allow to set in refrigerator at least 2 hours before loosely covering with waxed paper.

*If there are extra hazelnuts, dip them into the chocolate to be eaten separately.

Makes approximately 3 dozen.

Cognac Walnut Truffles

A real delight for lovers of crunchy walnuts, this truffle sandwiches creamy ganache between whole walnut halves before dipping.

> 6 *ounces semisweet chocolate*
> ¼ *cup heavy cream, room temperature*
> 1½ *Tablespoons cognac*
> 66 *walnut halves*
> ½ *cup finely chopped walnuts*

Chocolate Coating:
> 16 *ounces dark sweet chocolate*
> ¼ *cup vegetable oil*

 ## Ganache

Prepare ganache by chopping or grating chocolate into small pieces. Place in top half of double boiler along with cream. Put hot (not boiling) water in bottom of double boiler, making sure water doesn't touch top half. Stir with wooden spoon. When melted, beat until smooth. Remove from heat and let cool to room temperature.

When ganache is at room temperature, stir in cognac. Blend thoroughly. Transfer to covered bowl and refrigerate overnight to harden.

Taking two walnut halves at a time, sandwich a generous amount of filling between them. Place on waxed paper-lined baking sheet. Repeat with remaining ganache and walnuts. Refrigerate baking sheet overnight until truffles are firm. Allow to set in refrigerator at least 2 hours before loosely covering with waxed paper.

Dipping

Prepare chocolate coating with 16 ounces dark sweet chocolate and ¼ cup vegetable oil. Chop or grate chocolate into small pieces. Heat chocolate and oil together in top of double boiler over hot water, stirring with a wooden spoon until smooth. Insert candy thermometer and begin dipping when temperature registers between 85º-90ºF. If chocolate begins to cool and thicken before you're finished dipping, reheat over hot water.

Work with ½ dozen ganache balls at a time, keeping the rest refrigerated. Drop a ganache into the chocolate, turning until completely covered. Lift with fork, letting excess drain off, then gently rap fork against rim of pan to remove more chocolate. Using a butterknife gently slide truffle off of fork onto waxed paper-lined baking sheet. Repeat with remaining truffles.

Garnish

Sprinkle tops of truffles lightly with chopped walnuts. Refrigerate truffles overnight to harden. Allow to set in refrigerator at least 2 hours before loosely covering with waxed paper.

Makes approximately 30.

Chocolate Chip Truffles

Three layers of deep dark chocolate.

> 9 ounces semisweet chocolate
> 1 cup heavy cream, room temperature
> 3 ounces dark sweet chocolate, chopped into small chunks
> 1 Tablespoon Sabra Orange-Chocolate Liqueur®

Chocolate Coating:
> 16 ounces dark sweet chocolate
> ¼ cup vegetable oil
> 1 cup dark chocolate shavings

 Ganache

Prepare ganache by chopping or grating chocolate into small pieces. Place in top half of double boiler along with cream. Put hot (not boiling) water in bottom of double boiler, taking care that water doesn't touch top half. Stir with a wooden spoon. When melted, beat vigorously until smooth. Remove from heat and let cool to room temperature.

When ganache is at room temperature, add Sabra Liqueur and dark chocolate chunks, stirring until thoroughly blended. Transfer to covered bowl and refrigerate overnight to harden.

Taking a little ganache at a time, form 1" balls using fingertips (with as little contact as possible so chocolate doesn't soften). Keep unused portion refrigerated as you work. Place balls on waxed paper-lined baking sheet and refrigerate overnight until truffles are hardened. Allow to set in refrigerator at least 2 hours before loosely covering with waxed paper.

Dipping

Prepare chocolate coating with 16 ounces dark sweet chocolate and ¼ cup vegetable oil. Chop or grate chocolate into small pieces. Heat chocolate and oil together in top of double boiler over hot water, stirring with a wooden spoon until smooth. Insert candy thermometer and begin dipping ganache balls when temperature registers between 85⁰-90⁰F. If chocolate begins to cool and thicken before you're finished dipping, reheat over hot water.

Work with ½ dozen ganache balls at a time, keeping the rest refrigerated. Drop ganache into the chocolate, turning until completely covered. Lift with fork, letting excess drain off, then gently rap fork against rim of pan to remove more chocolate. Gently slide truffle off of fork (using a butter-knife) onto waxed paper-lined baking sheet. Repeat with remaining truffles.

Garnish

Garnish truffle by sprinkling dark chocolate shavings over top. Repeat with remaining truffles. Refrigerate truffles overnight or until firm. Allow to set in refrigerator at least 2 hours before loosely covering with waxed paper.

Makes approximately 40.

Champagne Buttercream Truffles

The most elegant truffle of them all.

   3 *Tablespoons sweet butter, softened*
1½ *cups powdered sugar*
   1 *teaspoon grated lemon zest*
   2 *Tablespoons dry champagne*

Chocolate Coating:
   16 *ounces white chocolate*
   ¼ *cup vegetable oil*
      a little dark dipping chocolate, either from
      another recipe or prepared fresh

 Ganache

Beat the butter until creamy, then gradually beat in sugar, champagne, and lemon zest. Beat another five minutes or until mixture is stiff and smooth. Refrigerate in a covered bowl overnight to harden.

Taking a little buttercream at a time, form 1" balls using fingertips (with as little contact as possible so chocolate doesn't soften). Keep unused portion refrigerated while you work. Place balls on waxed paper-lined baking sheet and refrigerate overnight until they are hardened. Allow to set in refrigerator at least 2 hours before loosely covering with waxed paper.

Dipping

Prepare chocolate coating with 16 ounces white chocolate and ¼ cup vegetable oil. Drop ganache into the chocolate, turning until completely covered. Lift with fork, letting excess drain off, then gently rap fork against rim of pan to remove more chocolate. Using a butterknife, gently slide truffle off of fork onto waxed paper-lined baking sheet. Repeat with remaining truffles.

 Garnish

To garnish, either reheat or mix up a fresh small amount of dark sweet chocolate coating. Be careful chocolate doesn't burn if you are only heating a small amount. Insert candy thermometer and when it registers 85°-90°F, dip fork into chocolate and quickly drizzle chocolate strings over each truffle. Refrigerate truffles overnight to harden. Allow to set in refrigerator at least 2 hours before loosely covering with waxed paper.

Makes approximately 20.

Orange Buttercream Truffles

This is a superb 3 part truffle, consisting of an orange buttercream center covered in chocolate ganache, then finally chocolate dipped. Although it takes longer to make, I think you'll find that it's worth the extra time.

>   5   *Tablespoons sweet butter, room temperature*
> 1½   *cups powdered sugar*
>   4   *Tablespoons grated orange zest*
>   2   *Tablespoons grated coconut*
>   1   *Tablespoon Kirsch®*
>   1   *Tablespoon fresh lemon juice*
> 10   *ounces semisweet chocolate*
>   1   *cup heavy cream, room temperature*
>   1   *Tablespoon Cointreau®*

Chocolate Coating:
> 16   *ounces dark sweet chocolate*
> ¼   *cup vegetable oil*
>   *candied orange peel for garnish*

 ## Center

Prepare orange buttercream by beating 3 Tablespoons of the butter until creamy. Slowly add sugar, orange zest, coconut, Kirsch, and lemon juice. Beat 5 minutes, or until stiff and smooth. Refrigerate in covered bowl at least 2 days to harden.

 ## Ganache

Prepare chocolate ganache by chopping or grating chocolate into small pieces. Place in top half of double boiler with cream and 2 Tablespoons butter. Put hot (not boiling) water in bottom of double boiler making sure water doesn't touch top half. Stir with wooden spoon. When melted, beat until well combined. Remove from heat, let cool to room temperature.

When ganache is at room temperature, add Cointreau, stirring until thoroughly blended. Transfer to covered bowl and refrigerate 2 days to harden.

Taking a little buttercream at a time, form 1" balls using fingertips (with as little contact as possible so mixture doesn't soften). Keep unused portion refrigerated as you work. Place balls on waxed paper lined baking sheet. Continue until buttercream is used up. Refrigerate baking sheet until centers are hardened, overnight. Allow to set in refrigerator at least 2 hours before loosely covering with waxed paper.

Working with ½ dozen truffles at a time, coat each buttercream center with a layer of chocolate ganache, molding gently with fingertips. Place each ½ dozen of these on a waxed paper-lined baking sheet and refrigerate immediately before coating the next batch. Repeat until all buttercream balls are coated. Refrigerate overnight waiting at least 2 hours before covering loosely with waxed paper.

Dipping

Prepare chocolate coating using 16 ounces dark sweet chocolate and ¼ cup vegetable oil. Chop or grate chocolate into small pieces. Heat chocolate and oil together in top half of double boiler over hot (not boiling) water, stirring with a wooden spoon until smooth. Insert thermometer and begin dipping when temperature registers 85°-90°F. If chocolate begins to cool and thicken before you're finished dipping, reheat over hot water.

Work with ½ dozen centers at a time, keeping the rest refrigerated. Drop center into the chocolate, turning until completely covered. Lift with fork, letting excess drain off, then gently rap fork against rim of pan to remove more chocolate. Using a butterknife, gently slide truffle off of fork onto waxed paper-lined baking sheet. Repeat with remaining truffles.

Garnish

Decorate truffles with criss-crossed slivers of candied orange peel. Refrigerate truffles overnight or until firm. Allow to set in refrigerator at least 2 hours before loosely covering with waxed paper.

Makes about 30.

Chocolate Truffles
with Amaretto Apricots

This truffle has a rich apricot buttercream center, a perfect partner for the dark chocolate shell.

> 6 *ounces plump dried apricots*
> ¾ *cup Amaretto*
> 4 *Tablespoons sweet butter, room temperature*
> 1¾ *cups powdered sugar*

Chocolate Coating:
> 16 *ounces dark sweet chocolate*
> ¼ *cup vegetable oil*
> 1 *cup whole blanched almonds*

 Center

For buttercream center: place apricots in saucepan, cover with water. Simmer for 5 minutes, then drain completely. Coarsely chop apricots. Transfer to small bowl and cover apricots with Amaretto. Refrigerate for an hour, turning apricots occasionally. Drain thoroughly then pat dry carefully. Save 2 Tablespoons of the liquid, discarding the rest.

To make buttercream, use mixer on medium speed to beat butter until fluffy. Add sugar gradually, then add reserved marinade. Beat another 5 minutes. Mix apricots gently into buttercream, then refrigerate mixture overnight to harden.

Take a little of the apricot/buttercream mixture at a time and form 1" balls using fingertips (with as little contact as possible so mixture doesn't soften). Keep unused portion refrigerated as you work. Place balls on waxed paper-lined baking sheet, continue until buttercream is used up. Refrigerate baking sheet overnight until truffles are hardened. Allow to set in refrigerator at least 2 hours before loosely covering with waxed paper.

 **Dipping**

Prepare chocolate coating with 16 ounces dark sweet chocolate and ¼ cup vegetable oil. Chop or grate chocolate into small pieces. Heat chocolate and oil together in top of double boiler over hot water, stirring with a wooden spoon until smooth. Insert candy thermometer and begin dipping when temperature registers 85°-90°F. If chocolate begins to cool and thicken before you're finished dipping, reheat over hot water.

Work with ½ dozen centers at a time, keeping the rest refrigerated. Drop a center into the chocolate, turning to coat completely. Lift with fork, letting excess drain off, then gently rap fork against rim of pan to remove more chocolate. Gently slide truffle off of fork onto waxed paper-lined baking sheet. Repeat with remaining truffles.

 Garnish

Hand dip each almond, holding it at one end and dipping just the tip in chocolate. Affix this black and white decoration to the top of each truffle. (If truffles have cooled too much by this time, spread a little warm chocolate on top with your finger before attaching almond.) Return baking sheet to refrigerator overnight. Allow truffles to set in refrigerator at least 2 hours before loosely covering with waxed paper.

Makes approximately 2 dozen.

Swiss Chocolate Cherry Truffles

Bearing little resemblance to conventional chocolate-covered cherries, this recipe wraps a sour cherry in chocolate ganache, before dipping.

> 8 *ounces dark sweet chocolate*
> ½ *cup heavy cream, room temperature*
> 1 *large can sour pitted cherries packed in water, drained thoroughly*
> 1½ *Tablespoons Cheri-Suisse® (chocolate/cherry liqueur)*

Chocolate Covering:
> 16 *ounces dark sweet chocolate*
> ¼ *cup vegetable oil*

 ## Ganache

Prepare ganache by chopping or grating chocolate into small pieces. Place in top half of double boiler along with cream. Put hot (not boiling) water in bottom of double boiler, making sure water doesn't touch top half. Stir with wooden spoon. When melted, beat until smooth. Remove from heat and let cool to room temperature.

When ganache is at room temperature, stir in Cheri-Suisse until thoroughly blended. Transfer to covered bowl and refrigerate overnight.

Drain cherries on paper towels for at least 20 minutes, and carefully pat dry. Taking a little ganache at a time, form a 1" ball around a single cherry, using fingertips (with as little contact as possible so chocolate doesn't soften). Repeat with remaining cherries. Keep unused portion refrigerated as you work. Place balls on waxed paper-lined baking sheet and refrigerate overnight until truffles are hardened. Allow to set in refrigerator at least 2 hours before loosely covering with waxed paper.

Prepare chocolate coating with 16 ounces dark sweet chocolate and ¼ cup vegetable oil. Chop or grate chocolate into small pieces. Heat chocolate and oil together in top of double boiler over hot water, stirring with a wooden spoon until smooth. Insert candy thermometer and begin dipping when temperature registers 85º-90ºF. If chocolate begins to cool and thicken before you're finished dipping, reheat over hot water.

Work with ½ dozen centers at a time, keeping the rest refrigerated. Drop a center into the chocolate, turning to coat completely. Lift with fork, letting excess drain off, then gently rap fork against rim of pan to remove more chocolate.

Gently invert truffle off of fork onto waxed paper-lined baking sheet. A string of chocolate will stick to your fork. Quickly manipulate it into a "C" shape. Repeat with remaining truffles. Refrigerate truffles overnight to harden. Allow to set in refrigerator at least 2 hours before loosely covering with waxed paper.

Makes approximately 30 truffles.

Cranberry Buttercream Truffles

A very special holiday treat: a marvelous mixture of tart cranberry, a hint of orange and lots of sweet buttercream and chocolate.

½ cup fresh cranberries, chopped
⅛ teaspoon lemon juice
1 Tablespoon sugar
1 Tablespoon grated orange zest
1 Tablespoon Hiram Walker Cranberry Cordial®
3 Tablespoons sweet butter, room temperature
1½ cups powdered sugar
9 ounces semisweet chocolate
¾ cup heavy cream, room temperature
1 teaspoon Cointreau®

Chocolate Covering:
16 ounces dark sweet chocolate
¼ cup vegetable oil

 Center

Put chopped cranberries in a small heavy saucepan with lemon juice and sugar. Cook over low heat for 5 minutes. Drain berries thoroughly and pat dry. Reserve 1 teaspoon of juice.

Prepare buttercream by beating butter until creamy. Slowly add powdered sugar, orange zest, and cranberry cordial. Beat 5 minutes or until stiff and smooth. Gently fold in cranberries. Refrigerate in a covered bowl overnight to harden.

 Ganache

Prepare chocolate ganache by chopping or grating chocolate into small pieces. Place in top half of double boiler along with cream. Put hot (not boiling) water in bottom of double boiler, making sure water doesn't touch top half.

Stir with wooden spoon. When melted, beat until smooth.

Remove from heat, let cool to room temperature. When ganache is at room temperature, add Cointreau and reserved juice stirring until well blended. Transfer to covered bowl and refrigerate overnight to harden.

Taking a little buttercream at a time, form 1" balls using fingertips (with as little contact as possible so mixture doesn't soften). Keep unused portion refrigerated as you work. Place balls on waxed paper-lined baking sheet, continuing until buttercream is used up. Refrigerate buttercream until centers are hardened, at least overnight. Allow to set in refrigerator at least 2 hours before loosely covering with waxed paper.

Working with ½ dozen centers at a time, coat each buttercream center with a layer of ganache, molding gently with fingertips. Place each ½ dozen of these on a waxed paper-lined baking sheet and refrigerate immediately before coating the next batch. Repeat until all buttercream balls are coated. Refrigerate overnight, waiting at least 2 hours before covering loosely with waxed paper.

 Dipping

Prepare chocolate coating using 16 ounces dark sweet chocolate and ¼ cup vegetable oil. Chop or grate chocolate into small pieces. Heat chocolate and oil together in top of double boiler over hot water, stirring with a wooden spoon until smooth. Insert thermometer and begin dipping when temperature registers 85º-90ºF. If chocolate begins to cool and thicken before you're finished dipping, reheat over hot water.

Work with ½ dozen centers at a time, keeping the rest refrigerated. Drop a single center into the chocolate, turning until completely covered. Lift with fork, letting excess drain off, then gently rap fork against rim of pan to remove more chocolate.

Gently invert truffle off of fork onto waxed paper-lined baking sheet. A strand of chocolate will stick to your fork. Quickly manipulate it into a zigzag shape atop the truffle. Repeat with remaining truffles. Refrigerate truffles overnight or until firm. Allow to set in refrigerator at least 2 hours before loosely covering with waxed paper.

Makes about 30.

Non-Alcoholic Truffles

For the folks who don't enjoy the taste of alcohol in their candies, here is a series of marvelous truffles which derive their flavors from ingredients such as fresh fruit, peanut butter, and a variety of spices.

Although alcohol figures prominently in the grand tradition of the truffle, many wonderful recipes containing no spirits have stood the test of time as gracefully as their alcohol-flavored counterparts.

Several of these classics are included here, as well as a number of my own invention. I feel sure that once you taste these, they'll be on your list of favorites.

Non-Alcoholic Truffles

Peanutbutter Meltaway Truffles

Better than any other combination of these classic ingredients.

> 6 ounces semisweet chocolate
> ¾ cup heavy cream, room temperature
> 3 Tablespoons chunky peanut butter, room temperature

Chocolate Coating:
> 16 ounces dark sweet chocolate
> ¼ cup vegetable oil
> 2 cups Spanish peanuts with skins removed, coarsely chopped

 **Ganache**

Prepare ganache by chopping or grating chocolate into small pieces. Place in top half of double boiler along with cream and peanut butter. Put hot (not boiling) water in bottom of double boiler, making sure water doesn't touch top half. Stir with wooden spoon. When melted, beat until smooth. Remove from heat and let cool to room temperature.

When ganache is at room temperature, transfer to covered bowl and refrigerate overnight to harden.

Taking a little ganache at a time, form 1" balls using fingertips (with as little contact as possible so chocolate doesn't soften). Keep unused portion refrigerated as you work. Place balls on waxed paper-lined baking sheet and refrigerate overnight until truffles are hardened. Allow to set in refrigerator at least 2 hours before loosely covering with waxed paper.

Dipping

Prepare chocolate coating with 16 ounces dark chocolate and ¼ cup vegetable oil. Chop or grate chocolate into small pieces. Heat chocolate and oil together in top of double boiler over hot water, stirring with a wooden spoon until smooth. Insert candy thermometer and begin dipping when temperature registers 85°-90°F. If chocolate begins to cool and thicken before you're finished dipping, reheat over hot water.

Work with ½ dozen ganache balls at a time, keeping the rest refrigerated. Drop ganache into the chocolate, turning until completely coated. Lift with fork, letting excess drain off, then gently rap fork against rim of pan to remove more chocolate. Gently slide truffle off of fork (using butterknife) onto waxed paper-lined baking sheet. Repeat with remaining truffles.

Garnish

Spread chopped nuts on another waxed paper-lined surface and gently roll each truffle (using fingertips) in nuts until completely coated. Return to baking sheet, repeat with remaining truffles. Refrigerate overnight to harden. Allow to set in refrigerator at least 2 hours before loosely covering with waxed paper.

Makes approximately 2 dozen.

Almond Chocolate Truffles

1½ cups almonds
6 ounces semisweet chocolate
1 egg yolk
2 Tablespoons heavy cream, room temperature

Chocolate Coating:
16 ounces dark sweet chocolate
¼ cup vegetable oil
½ cup unsweetened cocoa powder,
preferably Dutch® process

 ## Ganache

To prepare ganache, chop almonds very fine. Place grated or chopped chocolate, along with cream, in top of double boiler. Then put hot (not boiling) water in bottom pan, making sure water doesn't touch top pan. Stir with wooden spoon. When melted, beat until smooth. Stir in egg yolk and then almonds until well blended. Remove from heat and let cool to room temperature. Transfer to covered bowl and refrigerate overnight.

Taking a little ganache at a time, form 1" balls using fingertips (with as little contact as possible so chocolate doesn't soften). Keep unused portion in refrigerator as you work. Place balls on waxed paper-lined baking sheet and refrigerate overnight until truffles are hardened. Allow to set in refrigerator at least 2 hours before loosely covering with waxed paper.

Dipping

Prepare chocolate coating with 16 ounces dark sweet chocolate and ¼ cup vegetable oil. Chop or grate chocolate into small pieces. Heat chocolate and oil together in top of double boiler over hot water, stirring with a wooden spoon until smooth. Insert candy thermometer and begin dipping when temperature registers 85°-90°F. If chocolate begins to cool and thicken before you're finished dipping, reheat over hot water.

Work with ½ dozen ganache balls at a time, keeping the rest refrigerated. Drop ganache into the chocolate, turning until completely covered. Lift with fork, letting excess drain off, then gently rap fork against rim of pan to remove more chocolate. Gently slide truffle off of fork (with butterknife) onto waxed paper-lined baking sheet. Repeat with remaining truffles.

Garnish

Sift cocoa powder evenly over truffles to coat. Return baking sheet to refrigerator overnight or until truffles are firm. Allow to set in refrigerator at least 2 hours before loosely covering with waxed paper.

Makes approximately 2 dozen.

Lemon Chocolate Cheesecake Truffles

Based on a popular delicious cheesecake recipe which blends tangy lemon and rich, dark chocolate.

> *8 ounces semisweet chocolate*
> *3 ounce package cream cheese, softened*
> *1 cup heavy cream, room temperature*
> *1 Tablespoon lemon juice*
> *1 Tablespoon freshly grated lemon zest*

Chocolate Coating:
> *16 ounces dark sweet chocolate*
> *¼ cup vegetable oil*
> *2 cups graham cracker crumbs*

 Ganache

Prepare ganache by chopping or grating chocolate into small pieces. Place in top half of double boiler along with cream cheese and cream. Put hot (not boiling) water in bottom of double boiler, making sure water doesn't touch top half. Stir with wooden spoon. When melted, beat until smooth. Remove from heat, let cool to room temperature.

When ganache is at room temperature, beat in lemon juice and lemon zest. Transfer to covered bowl and refrigerate overnight.

Taking a little ganache at a time, form 1" balls using fingertips (with as little contact as possible so chocolate doesn't soften). Keep unused portion refrigerated as you work. Place balls on waxed paper-lined baking sheet and refrigerate overnight until truffles are hardened. Allow to set in refrigerator at least 2 hours before loosely covering with waxed paper.

Dipping

Prepare chocolate coating with 16 ounces dark sweet chocolate and ¼ cup vegetable oil. Chop or grate chocolate into small pieces. Heat chocolate and oil together in top of double boiler over hot water, stirring with a wooden spoon until smooth. Insert candy thermometer and begin dipping ganache balls when temperature registers between 85°-90°F. If chocolate begins to cool and thicken before you're finished dipping, reheat over hot water.

Work with ½ dozen ganache balls at a time, keeping the rest refrigerated. Drop ganache into the chocolate, turning until completely covered. Lift with fork, letting excess drain off, then gently rap fork against rim of pan to remove more chocolate. Gently slide truffle off of fork (using a butterknife) onto waxed paper-lined baking sheet. Repeat with remaining truffles.

Garnish

Garnish each truffle by rolling it in a pan of graham cracker crumbs until completely coated. Refrigerate on baking sheet overnight or until firm. Allow to set in refrigerator at least 2 hours before loosely covering with waxed paper.

Makes approximately 30.

Strawberry Cheesecake Truffles

The best of all possible worlds, a chocolate truffle with the flavors of the richest, creamiest cheese cake.

> 8 *ounces semisweet chocolate*
> 3 *ounce package cream cheese, softened*
> ¾ *cup heavy cream, room temperature*
> ⅛ *teaspoon lemon juice*
> 4 *ounces fresh strawberries, coarsely chopped*

Chocolate Coating:
> 16 *ounces dark sweet chocolate*
> ¼ *cup vegetable oil*
> 2 *cups graham cracker crumbs*

 Ganache

Wash strawberries and carefully pat dry. Prepare ganache by chopping or grating chocolate into small pieces. Place in top half of double boiler along with cream cheese and cream. Put hot, (not boiling) water in bottom of double boiler, making sure water doesn't touch top half. Stir with wooden spoon. When melted, beat until smooth. Remove from heat, let cool to room temperature. When ganache is at room temperature, gently fold in strawberries and lemon juice. Transfer to covered bowl and refrigerate overnight.

Taking a little ganache at a time, form 1" balls using fingertips (with as little contact as possible so chocolate doesn't soften). Keep unused portion refrigerated as you work. Place balls on waxed paper-lined baking sheet and refrigerate overnight until truffles are hardened. Allow to set in refrigerator at least 2 hours before loosely covering with waxed paper.

 **Dipping**

Prepare chocolate coating with 16 ounces dark sweet chocolate and ¼ cup vegetable oil. Chop or grate chocolate into small pieces. Heat chocolate and oil together in top of double boiler over hot water, stirring with a wooden spoon until smooth. Insert candy thermometer and begin dipping ganache balls when temperature registers between 85º-90ºF. If chocolate begins to cool and thicken before you're finished dipping, reheat over hot water.

Work with ½ dozen ganache balls at a time, keeping the rest refrigerated. Drop ganache into the chocolate, turning until completely covered. Lift with fork, letting excess drain off, then gently rap fork against rim of pan to remove more chocolate. Gently slide truffle off of fork (using a butter-knife) onto waxed paper-lined baking sheet. Repeat with remaining truffles.

 Garnish

Garnish each truffle by rolling it in a pan of graham cracker crumbs until completely coated. Return to baking sheet. Refrigerate truffles overnight or until firm. Allow to set in refrigerator at least 2 hours before loosely covering with waxed paper.

Makes approximately 30.

Black and White Truffles

For the serious chocoholic, a heavenly combination of dark and white chocolate chunks with creamy ganache.

> 8 *ounces dark sweet chocolate*
> 3 *ounces white chocolate, chopped coarsely into chunks*
> 1 *cup heavy cream, room temperature*

Chocolate Coating:
> 16 *ounces white chocolate*
> ¼ *cup vegetable oil*
> *chocolate sprinkles*

 Ganache

Prepare ganache by chopping or grating chocolate into small pieces. Place in top half of double boiler along with cream. Put hot (not boiling) water in bottom of double boiler, taking care that water doesn't touch top half. Stir with a wooden spoon. When melted, beat vigorously until smooth. Remove from heat and let cool to room temperature.

When ganache is at room temperature, fold in white chocolate chunks. Transfer to covered bowl and refrigerate overnight to harden.

Taking a little ganache at a time, form 1" balls using fingertips (with as little contact as possible so chocolate doesn't soften). Keep unused portion refrigerated as you work. Place balls on waxed paper-lined baking sheet and refrigerate overnight until truffles are hardened. Allow to set in refrigerator at least 2 hours before loosely covering with waxed paper.

Dipping

Prepare chocolate coating with 16 ounces white chocolate and ¼ cup vegetable oil. Chop or grate chocolate into small pieces. Heat chocolate and oil together in top of double boiler over hot water, stirring with a wooden spoon until smooth. Insert candy thermometer and begin dipping ganache balls when temperature registers 85°-90°F. If chocolate begins to cool and thicken before you're finished dipping, reheat over hot water.

Work with ½ dozen ganache balls at a time, keeping the rest refrigerated. Drop ganache into the chocolate, turning until completely covered. Lift with fork, letting excess drain off, then gently rap fork against rim of pan to remove more chocolate. Gently slide truffle off of fork (using a butter-knife) onto waxed paper-lined baking sheet. Repeat with remaining truffles.

Garnish

Roll each truffle in a pan of chocolate sprinkles until completely coated. Return to baking sheet. Refrigerate truffles until firm, or overnight. Allow to set in refrigerator at least 2 hours before loosely covering with waxed paper.

Makes approximately 3 dozen.

Bittersweet Mocha Truffles

For coffee lovers everywhere, the magic combination of chocolate and coffee is a guaranteed delight.

> 8 *ounces dark sweet chocolate*
> ¾ *cup heavy cream, room temperature*
> 1 *egg yolk*
> 3 *Tablespoons strong black coffee or espresso*

Chocolate Coating:
> 16 *ounces dark sweet chocolate*
> ¼ *cup vegetable oil*
> ½ *pound chocolate coffee beans or*
> *chocolate covered espresso beans* *

 **Ganache**

Prepare ganache by chopping or grating chocolate into small pieces. Place in top half of double boiler along with cream. Put hot (not boiling) water in bottom of double boiler, taking care that water doesn't touch top half. Stir with a wooden spoon. When melted, beat vigorously until smooth. Remove from heat and let cool to room temperature.

When ganache is at room temperature, add egg yolk and coffee. Stir until thoroughly blended. Transfer to covered bowl and refrigerate overnight to harden.

Taking a little ganache at a time, form 1" balls using fingertips (with as little contact as possible so chocolate doesn't soften). Keep unused portion refrigerated as you work. Place balls on waxed paper-lined baking sheet and refrigerate overnight until truffles are hardened. Allow to set in refrigerator at least 2 hours before loosely covering with waxed paper.

Dipping

Prepare chocolate coating with 16 ounces dark sweet chocolate and ¼ cup vegetable oil. Chop or grate chocolate into small pieces. Heat chocolate and oil together in top of double boiler over hot water, stirring with a wooden spoon until smooth. Insert candy thermometer and begin dipping ganache balls when temperature registers between 85⁰-90⁰F. If chocolate begins to cool and thicken before you're finished dipping, reheat over hot water.

Work with ½ dozen ganache balls at a time, keeping the rest refrigerated. Drop ganache into the chocolate, turning until completely covered. Lift with fork, letting excess drain off, then gently rap fork against rim of pan to remove more chocolate. Gently slide truffle off of fork (using a butter-knife) onto waxed paper-lined baking sheet. Repeat with remaining truffles.

Garnish

Top each truffle with a chocolate coffee bean or chocolate covered espresso bean. Refrigerate truffles overnight or until firm. Allow to set in refrigerator at least 2 hours before loosely covering with waxed paper.

* Either of these chocolate coffee bean candies should be available in most candy shops. They can also be found in gourmet mail order catalogs such as the *Madame Chocolate Catalog*.

Makes approximately 2 dozen.

Banana Creme Truffles

With the wonderful taste of fresh bananas, these fresh fruit truffles won't keep for long. Plan to use them up within a few days.

8 ounces semisweet chocolate
¾ cup heavy cream, room temperature
1 ripe banana, mashed
1 Tablespoon sweet butter, room temperature

Chocolate Coating:
16 ounces dark sweet chocolate
¼ cup vegetable oil
2 cups chopped walnuts

 Ganache

Prepare ganache by chopping or grating chocolate into small pieces. Place in top half of double boiler along with cream and butter. Put hot (not boiling) water in bottom of double boiler, taking care that water doesn't touch top half. Stir with a wooden spoon. When melted, beat vigorously until smooth. Remove from heat and let cool to room temperature.

When ganache is at room temperature, add banana. Beat until well blended. Transfer to covered bowl and refrigerate overnight to harden.

Taking a little ganache at a time, form 1" balls using fingertips (with as little contact as possible so chocolate doesn't soften). Keep unused portion refrigerated as you work. Place balls on waxed paper-lined baking sheet and refrigerate overnight until truffles are hardened. Allow to set in refrigerator at least 2 hours before loosely covering with waxed paper.

Dipping

Prepare chocolate coating with 16 ounces dark sweet chocolate and ¼ cup vegetable oil. Chop or grate chocolate into small pieces. Heat chocolate and oil together in top of double boiler over hot water, stirring with a wooden spoon until smooth. Insert candy thermometer and begin dipping ganache balls when temperature registers between 85º-90ºF. If chocolate begins to cool and thicken before you're finished dipping, reheat over hot water.

Work with ½ dozen ganache balls at a time, keeping the rest refrigerated. Drop ganache into the chocolate, turning until completely covered. Lift with fork, letting excess drain off, then gently rap fork against rim of pan to remove more chocolate. Gently slide truffle off of fork (using a butter-knife) onto waxed paper-lined baking sheet.

Garnish

Spread chopped nuts on another waxed paper-lined surface, and gently roll each truffle, using fingertips, in nuts until completely coated. Return to baking sheet; repeat with remaining truffles. Refrigerate overnight to harden. Allow to set in refrigerator at least 2 hours before loosely covering with waxed paper.

Makes approximately 2 dozen.

Pumpkin Pecan Truffles

A spicy holiday truffle that would complement any Thanksgiving feast.

> ¼ cup pumpkin pie filling
> ¼ teaspoon cinnamon
>   dash ground ginger
>   dash ground cloves
>   dash salt
> 1 Tablespoon sugar
> 8 ounces dark sweet chocolate
> ½ cup heavy cream, room temperature
> 1 egg yolk

Chocolate Coating:
> 16 ounces dark sweet chocolate
> ¼ cup vegetable oil
> 2 cups pecans, coarsely chopped

 **Ganache**

Place pumpkin pie filing in a bowl. Add cinnamon, ginger, cloves, salt, and sugar. Adjust spices to taste, taking care not to make the mixture too sweet.

Prepare ganache by chopping or grating chocolate into small pieces. Place in top half of double boiler along with cream. Put hot (not boiling) water in bottom of double boiler, taking care that water doesn't touch top half. Stir with a wooden spoon. When melted, beat vigorously until smooth. Remove from heat and let cool to room temperature. When ganache is at room temperature, add egg yolk and pumpkin mixture. Stir until well combined. Transfer to covered bowl and refrigerate overnight to harden.

Taking a little ganache at a time, form 1" balls using fingertips (with as little contact as possible so chocolate doesn't soften). Keep unused portion refrigerated as you work. Place balls on waxed paper-lined baking sheet and refrigerate overnight until truffles are hardened. Allow to set in refrigerator at least 2 hours before loosely covering with waxed paper.

 **Dipping**

Prepare chocolate coating with 16 ounces dark sweet chocolate and ¼ cup vegetable oil. Chop or grate chocolate into small pieces. Heat chocolate and oil together in top of double boiler over hot water, stirring with a wooden spoon until smooth. Insert candy thermometer and begin dipping ganache balls when temperature registers between 85°-90°F. If chocolate begins to cool and thicken before you're finished dipping, reheat over hot water.

Work with ½ dozen ganache balls at a time, keeping the rest refrigerated. Drop ganache into the chocolate, turning until completely covered. Lift with fork, letting excess drain off, then gently rap fork against rim of pan to remove more chocolate. Gently slide truffle off of fork (using a butterknife) onto waxed paper-lined baking sheet. Repeat with remaining truffles.

 Garnish

Spread chopped nuts on another waxed paper-lined surface, and gently roll each truffle, using fingertips, in nuts until completely coated. Return to baking sheet; repeat with remaining truffles. Refrigerate overnight to harden. Allow to set in refrigerator at least 2 hours before loosely covering with waxed paper.

Makes approximately 2 dozen.

Lemon Truffles

A welcome combination of tart lemon and sweet chocolate.

> 9 ounces semisweet chocolate
> ¾ cup heavy cream, room temperature
> 2 Tablespoons lemon juice
> 1 Tablespoon grated lemon zest

Chocolate Coating:
> 16 ounces dark sweet chocolate
> ¼ cup vegetable oil
> slivered lemon peel for garnish

 **Ganache**

Prepare ganache by chopping or grating chocolate into small pieces. Place in top half of double boiler along with cream. Put hot (not boiling) water in bottom of double boiler, taking care that water doesn't touch top half. Stir with a wooden spoon. When melted, beat vigorously until smooth. Remove from heat and let cool to room temperature.

When ganache is at room temperature, add lemon juice and lemon zest. Stir until thoroughly blended. Transfer to a covered bowl and refrigerate overnight to harden.

Taking a little ganache at a time, form 1" balls using fingertips (with as little contact as possible so chocolate doesn't soften). Keep unused portion refrigerated as you work. Place balls on waxed paper-lined baking sheet and refrigerate overnight until truffles are hardened. Allow to set in refrigerator at least 2 hours before loosely covering with waxed paper.

Dipping

Prepare chocolate coating with 16 ounces dark sweet chocolate and ¼ cup vegetable oil. Chop or grate chocolate into small pieces. Heat chocolate and oil together in top of double boiler over hot water, stirring with a wooden spoon until smooth. Insert candy thermometer and begin dipping ganache balls when temperature registers between 85°-90°F. If chocolate begins to cool and thicken before you're finished dipping, reheat over hot water.

Work with ½ dozen ganache balls at a time, keeping the rest refrigerated. Drop ganache into the chocolate, turning until completely covered. Lift with fork, letting excess drain off, then gently rap fork against rim of pan to remove more chocolate. Gently slide truffle off of fork (using a butter-knife) onto waxed paper-lined baking sheet. Repeat with remaining truffles.

Garnish

Top each truffle with a sliver of lemon peel for garnish. Refrigerate truffles overnight or until firm. Allow to set in refrigerator at least 2 hours before loosely covering with waxed paper.

Makes approximately 3 dozen.

Chestnut Buttercream Truffles

  3 Tablespoons sweet butter, softened
1½ cups powdered sugar
  1 teaspoon lemon juice
  1 Tablespoon syrup from chestnuts
  ¼ cup chestnuts in syrup, drained and coarsely
    chopped
  1 cup unsweetened cocoa powder, preferably
    Dutch® process

Beat butter until creamy. Slowly add sugar, lemon juice, and chestnut syrup. Beat 5 minutes, or until stiff and smooth. Gently fold in chestnuts. Refrigerate in a covered bowl several hours to harden.

Form 1" buttercream balls using fingertips, so mixture doesn't soften. Keep unused portion refrigerated as you work. Place balls on waxed paper-lined baking sheet. Refrigerate baking sheet until truffles are hardened, several hours or overnight. Shake 10-15 at a time in a plastic bag with as much cocoa as needed to coat completely. Repeat with remaining truffles.

Makes approximately 20.